GLOBAL CITIZENSHIP

Respecting Cultural Differences

A⁺

SUSAN WATSON

Smart Apple Media
1980 Lookout Drive
North Mankato
Minnesota 56003

Library of Congress Cataloging-in-Publication Data

Watson, Susan, 1949–
    Respecting cultural differences / by Susan Watson.
    p. cm — (Global citizenship)

    Includes index.
    Summary: Explores the many differences that exist between people throughout the world and what can be done to help reduce prejudice and discrimination and increase respect for cultural differences, both through government action and the efforts of individual citizens.
    Contents: Respecting the family—A world of differences—A world of cultural diversity—Respecting people's differences—Global citizens make a difference.

    ISBN 1-58340-400-7
    1. Toleration—Juvenile literature. 2. Ethnicity—Juvenile literature. 3. Pluralism (Social Sciences)—Juvenile literature.
    [1. Toleration. 2. Ethnicity. 3. Pluralism (Social Sciences) 4. World citizenship. 5. Globalization.] I. Title.
    HM1271.W39 2003
    305.8—dc21   2002044612

First Edition
9 8 7 6 5 4 3 2 1

First published in 2003 by
MACMILLAN EDUCATION AUSTRALIA PTY LTD
627 Chapel Street, South Yarra, Australia 3141

Associated companies and representatives throughout the world.

Copyright © Susan Watson 2003

Packaged for Macmillan Education Australia by Publishing Options Pty Ltd
Text design by Gail McManus Graphics
Cover design by Dimitrios Frangoulis
Illustrations by Infographics Pty Ltd
Page make-up by Crackerjack Desktop Services

Printed in Thailand

Acknowledgements
The author is especially grateful to Matthew, Kyja, CJ, and Samantha for being the model global citizens of this series. A special thanks to Dr Priscilla Clarke of the Free Kindergarten Association of Victoria for her advice on this title; to Lyn Pool for her photos of the families on pp. 6 and 7; and to the Sansom family (p. 6), the Tuara family (p. 7) and Nina and the Levin–Buckland family (p. 9) for their stories. The author and the publisher are grateful to the following for permission to reproduce copyright materials:

Cover photograph: family celebrating Kwanzaa, courtesy of Getty Images.

AAP/AP Photo/Richard Lewis, p. 17; Angela Berry, p. 21 (top); Jean-Marc La Roque/Auscape International, p. 11; B. Morandi/NF—HoaQui/Auscape International, p. 12; Australian Picture Library/Corbis, p. 18; Nigel Clements, p. 24 (top); Coo-ee Picture Library, pp. 10, 15, 19 (top), 23 (top); photos by Lyn Pool, courtesy of the Free Kindergarten Association, Victoria, pp. 6, 7 (top); Getty Images, pp. 4–5 (center), 8, 22 (bottom), 26 (top), 27, 28; Neil McLeod, p. 20; Reuters, pp. 13, 16, 25 (top), 29 (top); Susan Watson, pp. 4 (far left), 4 (center left), 5 (center right), 5 (far right), 9, 24 (bottom), 30; World Images, pp. 22–3 (center).

Please note
At the time of printing, the Internet addresses appearing in this book were correct. Owing to the dynamic nature of the Internet, however, we cannot guarantee that all these addresses will remain correct.

Global citizens   4
Global citizens respect
cultural differences 5

Respecting the family   6
◎ Different types of families 6

A world of differences   10
◎ Racial backgrounds 10
◎ Religions 12
◎ Ways of communicating 14
◎ Political systems 16
◎ Standards of living 18
◎ Social classes 19

A world of cultural diversity   20
◎ What is culture? 20
◎ All cultures celebrate 22

Respecting people's differences   26
◎ Accepting others 26
◎ Prejudice and discrimination 27

Global citizens make a difference   30
◎ Respecting cultural differences 30

Glossary   31
Index   32

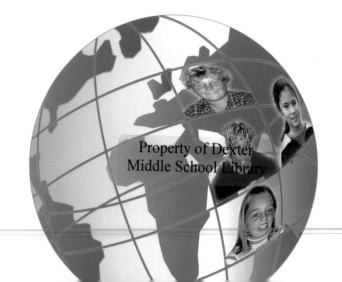

Global citizens

A global citizen is a person who:
◎ has rights and responsibilities
◎ acts in a caring way based on knowledge and understanding
◎ relates to others within their family, friendship groups, community, and country
◎ develops personal values and commitments
◎ develops a sense of their own role in the world.

A study of global citizenship will help you understand how people affect the quality of global environments and the well-being of others. Active global citizens do not just sit back and wait for others to do something. They turn their ideas into action. Action can take many forms:
◎ volunteering by giving time, help, and ideas freely
◎ talking to your friends
◎ thinking deeply
◎ learning more
◎ taking part in community events.

Throughout this book Allira, Harry, Lin, and Denzel will tell you their ways of acting as global citizens. We can all care for each other and our environment.

citizen
a person who lives in a large group of people who they mix with

environments
natural and built surroundings

ALLIRA

Hi! I'm Allira. I live in a country town near the sea. My family background is Aboriginal–Australian.

HARRY

Hello. I'm Harry. I live with my family in a suburb of a big modern city of four million people.

we are global citizens

People have many things in common. They all breathe, eat, drink, laugh, and cry. Everyone needs to have somewhere to live and play. They all have basic needs and wants in their everyday living.

People are also different from one another. They could be different in:

◎ the way they look
◎ the language they speak
◎ where they live
◎ the religion they follow
◎ the beliefs they have
◎ their ability to do things
◎ how they think about ideas and events
◎ the level of comfort in their everyday lives.

The world in which we live is full of such differences. Despite the differences, all people deserve to be treated with respect. Belonging to a particular group does not make one person better than another.

People are usually proud of their own families and communities. It is also important to respect other families and communities. Many people think that living in a world of differences makes life interesting.

religion
a set of sacred beliefs that a large number of people hold

respect
a high opinion of someone or something

LIN

I'm Lin. I migrated to my new country with my parents. We live with my grandparents who came 15 years ago from Malaysia.

We are global citizens

DENZEL

Hi! I'm Denzel. My mom and I live in a high-rise apartment close to the city center. We're African-American.

We can see differences in people all around us.

Different types of families

Families are valued in all countries around the world. All families have things in common. Family members help one another. They care about each other and are usually joined together by love.

There are also differences between families. They can differ in size, how they spend each day, and the traditions they value.

Nuclear families

Nuclear families usually have two adults and one or more children living at home together. They have other relatives who do not live with the nuclear family. Some nuclear families see their other relatives a lot, but others do not have strong attachments to them.

 A nuclear family

Our family is a nuclear family of me, as mom, my husband, and our two children. We all live together. My husband and I try to spend as much of our time as possible with the kids, especially while they are still not going to school full-time.

We want the children to grow up with lots of fresh air and fun.

Our nuclear family extends to the children's grandparents on both sides. We try to see them at least once a week. When my father retires from work, he is going to look after the children for one day a week while we are at work.

Some of our friends are African and Aboriginal people. It's just natural that the boys grow up drumming and dancing as part of our family life. We see this as the way of the future. With so many families from different backgrounds in our city, it's great that all of us have the pleasure of sharing our cultures together.

Extended families

Some families have relatives living in the same household. These are extended families. Other relatives could include the grandparents, aunts and uncles, and cousins. Each member of an extended family usually shares the household duties and bringing up the young children. They all pass on the family's traditions.

 CASE STUDY **Extended family**

Our family is from the Cook Islands in the southern Pacific Ocean near New Zealand. We came to live in New Zealand three years ago. We have a big family, and the children's uncle and two cousins all live with us.

As a family we do lots of shopping, especially going to the market. We buy plenty of fruit, chicken, and fish. We like to cook food in an earth oven.

My husband and I come from large families. I have six brothers and sisters. There are many nephews and nieces. My mom and dad live nearby so every weekend the family gathers for a picnic or grill.

My husband and I both work and share the parenting. I work during the day and my husband works on night shift. My brother and his two teenage kids live with us and they also help with childcare and household work.

What can I do?
There's a new kid in school from southern India.
I think he lives with lots of his relatives in an extended family.
I'll ask him over to our house after school so I can get to know
him better and learn how his family lives.

Single-parent families

Some children grow up in single-parent families where there is only a mother or father living at home. One parent might have died. One parent might have left the family household to start a new life somewhere else. A single mom may have decided not to marry nor live with the father of her children. Sometimes a woman has children, but does not want to raise them so the father decides to become a single dad.

In some countries such as Bosnia, Kosovo, Afghanistan, and Somalia, war has caused the death of a large number of married men. Single-parent mothers have to raise the children.

 CASE STUDY **Single-parent family**

ancestors
relatives from the past

generations
the difference in years between parents and children, usually 25 to 30 years

I live on my own with my two children. They've never known their father as he left when they were babies. He's never contacted us since then. My own parents have both died, so the kids don't have any grandparents.

I work full-time as a librarian. This doesn't leave me much time to spend with my children, but we make the most of our time together. They like school and stay on for two hours each day in the after-school program.

The weekends are busy. We do the shopping and housework together on Saturdays. My kids are a great help and keep their rooms clean. We have take-out on Saturday night. Then on Sundays we do something together outside our apartment, even if it's cold and raining. We spend lots of time in the park.

I want my children to be proud of our African ancestors. We are tracing our ancestors back through seven generations by doing our family tree.

Blended families

Today, more and more families are blended. A blended family is a mix of two different families. The mom and dad in a blended family often bring their own children from a previous relationship.

The parents could also have more children together in their new relationship. The parents and children in a blended family usually do lots of things together, but sometimes some of the brothers and sisters spend time with their other family too.

 A blended family

I'm Nina Levin. My immediate family is a blend of two families. Gary Buckland, the dad, already had two sons when we got together in our partnership. Josh Buckland is now 16 and Vince Buckland is 14. Gary and I have added to the family by having a daughter, Renata Levin-Buckland, who is three years old now. Our blended family is Nina, Gary, Josh, Vince, and Renata. We are all in the photo, except Josh who was in his room studying. Renata's teddy is also part of our family.

Josh and Vince spend their school week living at their mom's house. Their leisure time on most weekends is spent at our house. Gary does most of their washing and cooking. I'm not the boys' parent, but I give them lots of support. Sometimes I even help out when the boys are giving their dad a hard time! The responsibility of running our household is shared in all aspects.

Both of Renata's brothers help look after her and spend time playing with her. They even get into the sorts of little arguments that brothers and sisters always do.

My cultural background is Jewish. Gary and Vince are Christian, and Josh isn't religious. Our household respects both Jewish and Christian celebrations.

What can I do?

My mom is a single parent. But she's dating a real cool guy whose wife has died. He's got two kids a little bit younger than me. It will be awesome if we all get together in one big blended family!

Racial backgrounds

The people of the world come from a variety of different races. People of the same racial background are similar in their physical appearance. They have similar:

◎ skin color

◎ hair texture and color

◎ face, nose, and eyes shapes

◎ build and average height.

Under the skin, people are all the same. Even though the word "race" is sometimes used to show the differences between people, there is really only one race. This is the human race. Everybody is part of the human race.

races
very large groups of people who originated from the same places and have some physical characteristics in common

pigment
a substance that causes color

descendants
people today who are related to past generations of a particular family or group

People have different physical appearances, but everybody belongs to the human race, *Homo sapiens.*

 The color of people's skin

People's skin has cells with pigment. This pigment is called melanin. People with darker skin have more melanin than those with lighter skin. Melanin helps to protect the skin from the harmful rays of the sun. This is why the races of the world that have lived in hot, sunny places for thousands of years have dark skins.

Their descendants today are also usually dark skinned. People whose descendants are from colder places where the sun is less strong usually have fair skin.

Scientists have found that the color of a person's skin does not really make them different from others.

Different ethnic groups

For thousands of years, people have lived together in groups, tribes, clans, and communities. These groups are called ethnic groups. People in the same ethnic group have many things in common, especially their:

- race
- dance
- food
- celebrations
- family structure
- religion
- music
- beliefs
- traditional dress
- nationality.

Today, many people from different ethnic groups have moved away from their traditional homelands. They live in new countries to those of their ancestors. They still practice some of the traditions of their ethnic group in the new country.

In countries like the United Kingdom, Australia, the U.S., and Canada, there are people from many different ethnic backgrounds living side by side.

ethnic
special customs, beliefs, and characteristics of a group of people

traditional
relating to customs that have been practiced for hundreds or thousands of years

People in different ethnic groups often keep up their traditions even if they move to new countries.

What can I do?
My family now lives in Australia, but my ethnic background is Chinese from Malaysia. We still value the same things our family has for generations like celebrating Chinese New Year together.

Religions

Religion is important to many of the world's families. However, some people choose not to follow any religion at all.

Religion can affect the way people live. To some families, religion is the central force in their lives. Others may belong to a religion but it does not strongly influence their daily lives. They may only celebrate special religious occasions.

prophet
a person who tells what their god wants

Religious similarities

There are many different religions but most have these things in common:
◎ worship of a god or gods, or a special prophet
◎ worship through prayer
◎ a holy book
◎ distinctive symbols
◎ a place of worship where there are sacred statues
◎ a leader and special people to teach about the religion
◎ ceremonies to celebrate or honor special events
◎ a way of living that should be followed
◎ values of love, care for others, and the importance of the family.

Many religions also have particular forms of dress worn by the priests, ministers, teachers, and sometimes the followers themselves.

Jerusalem in Israel has many holy sites that are important to Jews, Christians, and some Muslims.

Religion	Place of worship	Holy book	Important symbol	
Christianity	church	Bible	cross and fish	
Judaism	synagogue	Torah	skull cap	
Islam	mosque	Koran	prayer mat	
Hinduism	mandir	Vedas	om/aum symbol	
Sikhism	gurdwara	Guru Granth Sahib	turban	
Buddhism	temple	Tripitaka	prayer beads	

Religious people often worship large statues, such as this one of Buddha.

The world's religions

About 86 percent of the world follows some sort of religion. The remaining 14 percent are not religious. More than two out of every three people in the world are Christian, Muslim (followers of Islam), or Hindu. Within the broad categories of most religions, there are denominations.

Indigenous peoples have their own religions that come from the place where the group belongs. Their religions generally connect them with nature, in particular the land, water, and the sun.

Christianity, Islam, and Judaism (the religion of Jewish people) are spread through many of the world's countries.

denominations
subsets of a religion

indigenous peoples
groups with the same language and culture who are related to the first people in an area

Top 10 countries

Rank	Christians Country	Followers	Muslims Country	Followers	Jews Country	Followers
1	U.S.	224,457,000	Indonesia	170,310,000	U.S.	5,602,000
2	Brazil	139,000,000	Pakistan	136,000,000	Israel	4,390,000
3	Mexico	86,120,000	Bangladesh	106,050,000	Russia	1,450,000
4	Russia	80,000,000	India	103,000,000	France	640,000
5	China	70,000,000	Turkey	62,410,000	Canada	350,000
6	Germany	67,000,000	Iran	60,790,000	U.K.	320,000
7	Philippines	63,470,000	Egypt	53,730,000	Argentina	250,000
8	U.K.	51,060,000	Nigeria	47,720,000	Brazil	150,000
9	Italy	47,690,000	China	37,108,000	Australia	92,000
10	France	44,150,000	Russia	27,000,000	South Africa	70,000

Ways of communicating

People communicate with each other in a range of different ways. The most important aspect of communication is language. Language is used in speech and writing. We learn to speak from a very early age, then we learn to read and write.

Languages of the world

language family
a broad group of similar languages that have come from a common ancestor

Every language belongs to a language family. There are about 3,500 different language families in the world today. Some have many millions of speakers. Other language families have fewer than 100 speakers. In fact, 60 percent of the world's languages have fewer than 10,000 speakers.

The top 12 languages in the world each have more than 100 million speakers using it as their main language. Mandarin (Chinese) ranks highest of these languages. Many people speak more than one language. They may use one language at home in their family group and another at school or work. People who have contact with different countries and speak more than two languages are multilingual.

GLOBAL FACT

Nearly two billion people speak English as their second language. This makes it the world's main second language.

Gelukkige nuwe jaar (Afrikaans)
Felices ano Nuevo (Argentinian)
Bon Any Nou! (Catalan)
Glaedelig nytar (Danish)
Gelukkig Nieuw Jaar (Dutch)
Happy New Year (English)
Head uut aastat! (Estonian)
Onnellista uutta vuotta! (Finnish)
Bonne Année! (French)
Hauoli Makahiki Hou! (Hawaiian)
Chena tova (Hebrew)
Selamat Tahun Baru! (Indonesian)
Yeni Yiliniz Kutlu Olsun (Turkish)
Giang Sing vui ve (Vietnamese)

"Happy New Year" in 14 different languages.

Rank	Language
1	Mandarin
2	English
3	Spanish
4	Arabic
5	Hindi
6	Portuguese
7	Bengali
8	Russian
9	French
10	Japanese
11	German
12	Bahasa

What's in a name?

Everyone has one or more names. Names identify a person and help us communicate with each other. In some communities, names have special meanings that are often associated with nature, personal strengths, religious beliefs, or the time of birth.

Non-verbal communication

Non-verbal communication does not use speech. Non-verbal communication covers:

◎ writing
◎ symbols
◎ hand gestures
◎ facial expressions
◎ eye contact
◎ sign language
◎ instruments that can be beaten, such as drums
◎ special codes used over radio waves
◎ flag signals.

GLOBAL FACT

Most countries have their own signing language. In the U.S., it is ASL (American Signing Language).

Non-verbal communication is used for a range of reasons where speech is not suitable or available. A person who cannot hear or speak uses special signing language made by their fingers, hands, lips, and other body movements.

In traditional communities, sign languages allowed different groups to communicate with each other. The Plains Indians of North America did this. Groups that hunt in the wild use sign language between hunters so that they do not scare the animals. Traditional Australian-Aboriginal peoples, and the peoples of Sudan and the Sahara use sign language like this.

Dance is another form of non-verbal communication that some groups use for special messages.

CASE STUDY **Maori Haka**

Haka is Maori dancing where the men dance at the front and the women sing behind them. The dance is important to New Zealand's Maoris as it communicates the group's identity with their indigenous background. Traditionally, the dance communicated important events and feelings in the welcoming and entertainment of visitors.

Today, Maori groups perform their Haka at the start of important events. It is performed at every All Blacks rugby game.

Political systems

There are about 195 countries in the world. Each has its own political system. Not all political systems are the same. There are differences in the laws from country to country. There are different ideas about how to run a country.

The main political systems in the world are democracy, dictatorship, monarchy, and communism.

political system
the laws and actions of running a country

government
the people who run a country

political party
a group of people with similar ideas about running a country

dictator
a leader of government that does not allow individual freedom or fair elections

Democracy

A democracy is a political system where all the citizens of a country are given the power to vote for the members of government. In a democracy, there is usually more than one political party wanting to run the country.

Within the laws of the country, democracy allows people the freedom to:
◎ have a say
◎ expect fair treatment
◎ participate in decisions
◎ act on their ideas.

Some of the countries of the world that are democracies are Germany, Australia, the U.S., India, South Africa, and Chile.

Dictatorship

A dictatorship is the opposite of a democracy. The government usually has not been elected by all of the citizens. The people in power have taken control, often by military force. There is only one main political group. The leader is a dictator.

Some of the countries of the world that are dictatorships are Burma (Myanmar), Sudan, and Libya.

In democracies people are allowed to meet in public places to express their ideas.

Monarchy

A monarchy is a political system where there is a king or queen as the head of government. The monarchy is passed down through the same family from one generation to the next. In Islamic countries, the monarch is a sultan and the system is a sultanate.

Monarchies can be part of a democracy. The monarch does not have as much power as the elected government. However, there are some monarchies or sultanates that have total control. They do not allow other political groups to form. They are similar to dictatorships.

The United Kingdom, the Netherlands, Japan, and Cambodia are democratic countries with a monarch. Saudi Arabia and Brunei are sultanates that do not allow democratic elections.

monarch
a king or queen

Queen Elizabeth II is one of the world's best-known monarchs. Since 1952, she has been queen of the United Kingdom, which has a democratic government.

Communism

A communist government believes that the whole society is more important than people's individual rights. In a one-party communist country, the government controls most things, even businesses and cultural activities.

Some people say that one-party communism is like a dictatorship. It is not easy for citizens to criticize their government or stand against them in elections. Religion is often forbidden. It is not usual for the average person to be able to own land or houses.

Some democracies have a ruling government with members from a communist party as well as other parties.

Some countries where one-party communism is practiced are Cuba, North Korea, China, Vietnam, and Laos. Other countries, such as Italy and France, have communist party members in their elected government.

GLOBAL FACT

Russia became the world's first communist nation in 1917 after a people's revolution against the monarch, Tsar Nicholas II.

revolution
a riot that overthrows the ruling government and replaces it with a new one

Standards of living

There are differences in how people are able to live. These differences occur across the world because of wealth. There are very rich people in most of the world's countries. There are also very poor people. Some countries have a high number of poor people who do not get enough of their basic needs.

Developed and developing countries

The United Nations is an international organization that tries to help the world become more peaceful. It is also concerned with the differences in the standard of living between countries. UNICEF is the United Nations Children's Fund. In 2001, UNICEF listed countries in two groups to show the differences in wealth between them. (Some countries are not listed as UNICEF does not have enough information about them.)

◎ The 31 developed countries are mostly in the northern hemisphere. Most of the countries of Europe and North America are developed. The two developed countries in the southern hemisphere are Australia and New Zealand.

◎ The 151 developing countries are located in Africa, South America, most of Asia, and the island nations of the Pacific and Indian Oceans.

UNICEF classifies India as a developing country. A large number of the people in India have a low standard of living, but there are many wealthy families as well.

wealth
the amount of money and comforts that a person or country has

standard of living
everyday living conditions in a community

developed countries
countries with a high standard of wealth and comforts for most people

northern hemisphere
the half of the globe above the equator

developing countries
countries with much lower standards of wealth and comfort than developed countries

GLOBAL FACT
A child born today in a developing country has a 4 out of 10 chance of living in extreme poverty.

Social classes

People can be separated in their own communities by social class such as:

◎ Upper-class people are usually very rich. They control businesses, own land and houses, expensive cars, and luxury items. They often have a lot of power.

◎ Middle-class people usually have well-paid jobs and regular work. They have a good level of wealth and comforts. They often send their children to private school and college.

◎ Working-class people are referred to as the "lower class." If they are able to get a job, it is often hard work in factories or outdoors. They have to struggle to provide for their family.

social class different levels of wealth, education, and land ownership in a society

caste system the different levels of social class in traditional Indian society

 CASE STUDY India's traditional caste system

The **caste system** has been part of India's social class system for about 3,500 years. Although modern Indian society is changing, the values of the caste system are still held strongly by some people. There are five different levels of the system:

• Brahman—priests
• Kshatriya—rulers, warriors, landowners
• Vaishya—business owners
• Shdra—farmers, craftspeople
• Harijans—those outside the system (the extremely poor and unwanted).

Traditionally, Indian people were born into one of the five castes, and had to marry and die in it. Those who were born into the very poor lower caste remained that way for generation after generation. The caste system is now not law, but many communities still practice it.

What can I do?

There's a type of social class system in my country. Some kids think that I'm not as good as they are because of my Aboriginal background. But I'm proud of my heritage. There wouldn't be a class system at all if we could respect each other's differences.

Global Citizenship

A world of cultural diversity

What is culture?

People live in groups that share a common culture. Groups can be families, local neighborhoods, ethnic, religious, or part of a particular region of a country.

Everybody belongs to a culture, no matter where they live. Many countries have a variety of different cultural groups in them. Culture has three special features:

◎ Culture is people's values. Most cultures consider family life, teaching young children, getting along with others, and keeping safe as very important.

◎ Culture is learned. From an early age, children look, listen, and learn what is valued in their families and communities. This learning continues through their school years into adulthood. They also learn culture from the wider community through TV, music, dance, and social occasions.

◎ Culture is shared. People share their culture with others, such as their family, neighborhood, or special group. They share beliefs and daily living practices. They also share language and non-verbal ways of communicating.

culture
the beliefs, values, and customs of a particular group of people

values
the ideas and behavior that a group wants its members to follow

Many cultures have a form of horoscope to tell the future, but each culture represents it in a different way. This is the Chinese wheel horoscope.

Storytelling and drawing are important in many cultures. Young children learn about their culture through these activities.

What is cultural diversity?

Think how many kinds of T-shirts, music CDs, or books there are. Or the many types of houses and cars that exist. Or the wonderful variety of animals, birds, fish, and plants all over the world. This is known as diversity.

Everyone has their own individual character. Everyone is different from others in some ways. Although people all belong to the human race, they show a great deal of diversity. There is also a lot of cultural diversity in the world. Cultural diversity is found in the different types of:

diversity
the range of different things

cultural diversity
the variety of cultural backgrounds in the world's people

◎ families
◎ food
◎ music
◎ art
◎ housing
◎ ethnic backgrounds
◎ festivals and celebrations
◎ languages
◎ religions
◎ ideas and opinions.

Cultural diversity is similar to biodiversity in the natural environment. Biodiversity occurs where there is a large range of living things, such as plants, animals, birds, and sea creatures living in particular habitats. When there is a lot of diversity in the natural environment, it is healthy and will be able to sustain itself into the future.

Many people believe that cultural diversity adds to the richness of the world. Cultural diversity helps people respect the contribution that each different individual and group makes to the world.

The different festivals that people celebrate are part of the world's cultural diversity.

What can I do?

Harry, Allira, Denzel, and I all have different cultural backgrounds. That means we've added to the cultural diversity of this book. And we're proud of it!

All cultures celebrate

Every culture shares the need to celebrate and honor special occasions. The special occasion can be celebrated within the family or with the wider community. The occasion might be:

◎ happy or sad
◎ religious
◎ a national day
◎ based on an old tradition or custom
◎ for a birth, death, marriage, or a stage in growing up
◎ in memory of war
◎ victory in a sporting, artistic, or other event.

There are many different ways of celebrating, but there are also similarities:

◎ Families involve lots of relatives to celebrate together.
◎ Often, a group larger than a family shares in the celebration.
◎ People often dress up in special clothes for the occasion. In India and China, white is worn at funerals. Black is usually worn at a Christian funeral. White is the traditional color for the bride's gown in Christian and Jewish wedding ceremonies. Hindu, Sikh, and Muslim brides wear red and gold.
◎ Decorations, flowers, and symbols are displayed or worn by people. In Hindu celebrations, multi-colored flower petals are scattered everywhere. In the U.S. streamers and floating colored paper pieces are used in street processions to celebrate victorious occasions.
◎ There is usually special food prepared.
◎ Candles, lights, fires, and fireworks feature in many celebrations. Light is a symbol of hope for the future.

Kwanzaa is a week-long celebration where many African-Americans honor their heritage. This family is dressed in traditional clothes for the celebration.

Chinese New Year celebrations last for two weeks in January or February each year. On the last day, dragon and lion dancers perform in the street accompanied by the sounds of drums, cymbals, flutes, and firecrackers. People wear red for good luck.

New Year celebrations

The start of a new year is celebrated in almost every culture. However, it is not always held at the same time. Different cultures have different calendars and ways of working out when the new year falls.

New Year celebrations symbolize a new beginning. It is a time to remember the year that has passed and to make changes for the coming year. Most people want the first day of the new year to be good; then the rest of the year should be good too.

In the cultures that see the new year in on the last night in December, families hold parties that go on past midnight. As midnight strikes, people blow hooters, throw streamers, whistle, and whoop. Then everyone shouts "Happy New Year," and hugs and kisses the people near them.

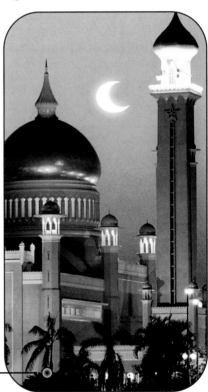

Islamic New Year is celebrated when the new crescent moon is seen in the sky.

Fireworks light up special occasions and bring hope for the future.

What can I do?
My new neighbors are from Ho Chi Minh City. They are Vietnamese. They've asked my family to share their Tet festival to celebrate new year. I'll take some tangerines as they are a symbol of good luck in their culture.

christening
a baptism or
naming ceremony
in the Christian
church

godparents
relatives or friends
who agree to
bring up a child if
the parents die

circumcised
where the foreskin
of a penis is cut

Birth celebrations

More than 75 million babies are born in the world every year. Birth is an important occasion in most cultures and is honored in different ways.

In Christian families, when the newborn child is only a few months old, a special christening service is held. This is usually in a church with a minister. The family, relatives, and friends gather in the church. The minister baptizes the child by brushing water over their head and giving the child a name. The child is given godparents as well.

Jewish baby boys are circumcised eight days after their birth in a ceremony called *Brit Milah* or "Ceremony of Cutting." The mother does not attend.

Birth is an important occasion that is celebrated by special ceremonies such as this Jewish *Brit Milah*.

Cemeteries are part of many cultures. They are where people are buried after they die.

In the Hindu ceremony *Samskar*, the newborn baby is washed and the sacred *Aum* symbol is traced on the tongue. The baby is named 12 days later.

Death ceremonies

Most cultures also hold a special service for someone who has died. Family, friends, and other people gather to hear speeches about the person who has died. It is often a sad occasion. But to many people it is also one of hope and joy. They believe the spirit of the person will go on to a better life beyond the physical world, especially if they have lived a good life.

In many cultures, the dead body is either buried in the ground in a cemetery or burned. When a body is burned, the ashes can be put in an urn and either buried or kept in a special family place.

Harvest festivals

Another type of celebration many cultures enjoy is the harvest festival. This takes place at the same time every year in each culture. People give thanks for the food that they have grown and eaten in the past year.

All the decorations displayed at harvest festivals are symbols of Earth's produce. People give thanks for every type of fruit and vegetable, and also for fish from the sea. There are different sorts of harvest festivals.

North Americans celebrate Thanksgiving on the fourth Thursday in November. They give thanks for the harvest gathered by the Pilgrims who settled there in 1620. This was when the Pilgrims shared their thanks with local Native Americans. The indigenous people had shown the European Pilgrims how to catch wild turkeys and grow sweet corn, sweet potatoes, pumpkins, and cranberries.

In Australia, New Zealand, and the United Kingdom, the festival takes place in early fall when many of the summer crops have been picked.

In Nigeria, people have celebrated *Argungu* or the "Fishing Festival" for over 400 years. They wear clothes with fish patterns on them. There is a fishing competition where the competitors use only a pumpkin-like shell and two nets.

Pacific Islanders celebrate the harvesting of their crops—in particular, yams. A yam is a potato-like plant that is a staple crop in many Pacific Island countries. If Islanders live near the sea, they also give thanks for the products of the sea.

Harvest festivals give thanks for the fruit and vegetables picked and fish taken from the sea.

staple crop
a main type of food of a group of people

Accepting others

People who treat others as individuals who have their own values and cultural backgrounds show respect for them. Respect for one another means valuing human diversity. It means accepting people's differences, even if they:

◎ look different
◎ have different colored skin
◎ are much older or younger
◎ practice a different religion
◎ speak a different language
◎ have different political ideas
◎ have a different standard of living
◎ celebrate special occasions differently
◎ live in a different country.

Respect does not mean that all behavior should be accepted. Disrespect is the opposite of respect. Behavior that comes from disrespect can lead to deliberate hurt or damage. Someone who is acting mean or bullying another person does not deserve respect. If a person breaks the rules of society by stealing or lying, they also do not deserve respect.

Respect is accepting people for who they are, as long as their behavior deserves respect. Respect also means treating people the way you expect to be treated by others.

Respect means accepting that other people's values and behavior can exist alongside your own.

What can I do?
It's easy to accept others if they show respect to you as well. I'll start showing others that I respect them by smiling and saying: "Hi, how are you?". I'll take the first step.

Prejudice and discrimination

The world is rich in cultural diversity, but not everyone sees diversity as a positive thing. Someone who does not appreciate diversity could even be afraid of it. Perhaps they do not know how to handle the differences around them. They could even develop a prejudice against others.

Examples of prejudice

Do you, or people that you know, ever make statements that start like these?

"All of those old women over there..."

"Every white person is . . . "

"That person in a wheelchair can't..."

"Girls are always..."

"Poor people are..."

"Vietnamese people all look the same so they..."

"That man's bald..."

---

prejudice
an opinion formed about someone or something because they are different

discrimination
the unfair treatment of people because they are considered different

Prejudice that is negative builds walls between people. It makes people judge other people unfairly. Prejudice against people can lead to action that is unfair and sometimes violent. Discrimination is a harmful action that often results from prejudice.

Before 1990, in South Africa, there was a system that discriminated against black people. They were not allowed to share public spaces, such as beaches, with white people.

Racial discrimination

Prejudice against people because of their different ethnic backgrounds or appearances can lead to racial discrimination.
These are examples of acts of racial discrimination:

◎ thinking that one race is better than another in intelligence, at particular jobs, or other activities

◎ when one group thinks that they are a "superior" race and people from other races should live and be educated apart

◎ when a person thinks they own their country and they want to keep other people from different races out.

Gender discrimination

gender
whether a person is male (boy, man) or female (girl, woman)

To discriminate against people because of their gender is known as gender discrimination. It is also called sex discrimination. Gender discrimination can take different forms, such as:

◎ girls not being allowed to attend school after an early age because they have to help with home duties

◎ girls being forced into a life of slavery where they must do what men tell them to do

◎ girls and women who work but who have to give all their money to the men in the family

◎ men who are thought to be a "sissy" because they work in jobs such as being a nurse.

Gender discrimination can affect both females and males if they work in jobs traditionally done by the opposite sex, such as nursing or science.

Other forms of discrimination

There are also other reasons why people discriminate against other people. These are based on prejudices against others who are different in some way, such as by:

◎ **Religion**—Many people think of Christianity, Judaism, Islam, Buddhism, and Hinduism as the world's religions. In fact, there are many others. Throughout history, there has always been unfair treatment of one religious group by another. This still continues in some places.

◎ **Class**—History has also shown that people in higher classes of society often discriminate against those less well-off. Upper-class people sometimes expect that lower-class people will do the hardest and dirtiest jobs. They may even stop people from lower classes from trying to get better standards of wealth.

This girl has been blind from birth. She joins in activities with other girls who are not blind.

◎ **Age**—Some people think that older people cannot do things as well as younger people, or think as quickly as them. Discrimination against older people might mean that they are forced to stop working before they want to. They are not given the chance of getting a job if someone younger is available.

◎ **Ability**—People's ability to do and think things is not always the same. A person could be physically or mentally disabled. Their ability limits them from doing the same things as many other people.

◎ **Physical appearance**—People's body shapes and looks vary greatly. Some people discriminate against those whose bodies and looks may not fit their ideas of good looks.

What can I do?
When I see someone who's not like me, my first reaction is to stay away from them. But I've just made friends with this kid who's got a crippling muscular disease. He's really cool. All kids need friends. We're not that different after all.

Respecting cultural differences

We all should be able to live in a world of differences. We should be proud of our own families and communities but, at the same time, respect that there are families and communities who may be different from ours.

All these differences will help make the world a more interesting and sustainable place in which to live.

We are all citizens of the world. But some of us are more active than others. We do not just have ideas but we put our words and ideas into action. Some people think that "action" means protesting or doing something violent. But action can take many forms and can always be peaceful, even in a protest march.

These are some actions that can help make a difference:
◎ keeping informed about events and telling others
◎ thinking deeply about issues
◎ volunteering and participating in community activities
◎ helping out wherever you can
◎ standing up for others
◎ joining groups that care about the environment and people
◎ using less in your day-to-day life
◎ reusing and recycling
◎ joining others on a Web site to lodge petitions
◎ discussing and solving problems in peaceful ways.

Remember: an idea is only an idea until someone puts it into action.

What can we do?
Global citizens discuss global issues to try to find ways of solving them. There is hope for the planet if we all act together.

ancestors relatives from the past

caste system the different levels of social class in traditional Indian society

christening a baptism or naming ceremony in the Christian church

circumcised where the foreskin of a penis is cut

citizen a person who lives in a large group of people who they mix with

cultural diversity the variety of cultural backgrounds of the world's people

culture the beliefs, values, and customs of a particular group of people

denominations subsets of a religion

descendants people today who are related to past generations of a particular family or group

developed countries countries with a high standard of wealth and comforts for most people

developing countries countries with much lower standards of wealth and comforts than developed countries

dictator a leader of government that does not allow individual freedom or fair elections

discrimination the unfair treatment of people because they are considered different

diversity the range of different things

environments natural and built surroundings

ethnic special customs, beliefs, and characteristics of a group of people

gender whether a person is male (boy, man) or female (girl, woman)

generations the difference in years between parents and children, usually 25 to 30 years

godparents relatives or friends who agree to bring up a child if the parents die

government the people who run a country

indigenous peoples groups with the same language and culture who are related to the first people in an area

language family a broad group of similar languages that have come from a common ancestor

monarch a king or queen

northern hemisphere the half of the globe above the equator

pigment a substance that causes color

political party a group of people with similar ideas about running a country

political system the laws and actions of running a country

prejudice an opinion formed about someone or something because they are different

prophet a person who tells what their god wants

races very large groups of people who originated from the same places and have some physical characteristics in common

religion a set of sacred beliefs that a large number of people worship

respect a high opinion of someone or something

revolution a riot that overthrows the ruling government and replaces it with a new one

social class different levels of wealth, education, and land ownership in a society

standard of living everyday living conditions in a community

staple crop the main type of food of a group of people

traditional relating to customs that have been practiced for hundreds or thousands of years

values the ideas and behavior that a group wants its members to follow

wealth the amount of money and comforts that a person or country has

A
active citizens 4, 30
ancestors 8

B
babies 24
birth 24
blended families 9
Buddhism 12, 29

C
castes 19
celebrations 22–5
cemeteries 24
Christianity 12, 13, 24, 29
class 19, 29
communicating 14–15
communism 17
culture 20–1

D
dance 15
death 24
democracy 16
descendants 10
developed countries 18
developing countries 18
dictatorship 16
discrimination 27–9
diversity 5, 21, 26, 27, 30

E
ethnicity 11, 21
extended families 7

F
families 6–9
freedom 16

G
gender discrimination 28
generations 8
global citizens 4
gods 12
government 16

H
harvest 25
Hinduism 12, 13, 24, 29
holy books 12
Homo sapiens 10

I
indigenous peoples 13
Islam 12, 13, 17, 23, 29

J
Jewish 13, 24
Judaism 12, 13, 24, 29

L
language 14

M
monarchy 17
Muslim *see* Islam

N
names 14, 24
New Year 14, 23
nuclear families 6

P
political systems 16
poverty 18, 19
prejudice 27

R
race 10, 28
religion 5, 9–12, 13, 17, 29
respect 5, 26

S
sex discrimination 28
sign language 15
Sikhism 12
single-parent families 8
skin color 10
speaking 14
standard of living 18
stepchildren 9
sultan 17

T
Thanksgiving 25
traditions 11, 15

U
UNICEF 18
United Nations 18

V
values 20
volunteering 4, 30

W
war 8
wealth 18, 19
worship 12
writing 14